# HADAKA-JIMI

*The Core Technique for*

## PRACTICAL UNARMED COMBAT

---

## MOSHE FELDENKRAIS, D.SC.

## PREFACE, AFTERWORD, FOOTNOTES, AND ADDITIONAL PHOTOS
## BY MOTI NATIV

Genesis II Publishing
Longmont, Colorado
AchievingExcellence.com

Feldenkrais, Moshe, 1904-1984.
Practical Unarmed Combat / by Moshe Feldenkrais © 1942

Updated with a new foreword by Moti Nativ, and updated photos and
resources.

*Feldenkrais®, Feldenkrais Method®, Functional Integration®,* and *Awareness
Through Movement®,* are Service marks of The *Feldenkrais* Guild®

Published by Genesis II Publishing, Inc.
Longmont, CO 80502
AchievingExcellence.com

Printed in the United States of America

ISBN: 978-1-884605-25-3

CIP: 2009930056

Michel Silice Feldenkrais (1953-2009)

My dear friend Michel dedicated his life to the promotion of the *Feldenkrais Method*. He wholeheartedly supported this publication by providing a wealth of historical materials, clever advice, and his abiding respect for the *Feldenkrais Method* and the memory of his uncle, Moshe.

I'm honored to dedicate the new edition of *Practical Unarmed Combat* to the memory of Michel Silice Feldenkrais.

# PRAISE FOR HADAKA-JIME: PRACTICAL UNARMED COMBAT

Dr. Moshe Feldenkrais was a remarkable man; teacher, soldier, researcher, judoka, visionary, martial artist, physicist, and pioneer. He was a founder of the European Judo Union, and respected by Gunji Koizumi, Mikinosuke Kawaishi, and Jigoro Kano. I therefore consider it an honour and a privilege to have been asked to write an endorsement to the new edition of his important text.

I met Moti Nativ when he visited the Bowen History of Judo Archive at University of Bath to continue his research into the life and work of Moshe Feldenkrais. I was immediately struck by his passion and commitment, and his depth of understanding into the relationship of mind and body as applied to Budo.

For me this book speaks on three levels. It is a treatise of an effective course of unarmed combat which has withstood the test of time. It is also an important document of social and cultural history when considered in the context that it was written. Thirdly it provides a level of insight for the advanced follower of the *Feldenkrais Method*® into the early thought processes of the founder.

Moti Nativ and Genesis II Publishing are to be commended for reminding us about the relevance of this text, and sharing with us the thoughts of a remarkable man.

— *Dr. Mike Callan, President, The International Association of Judo Researchers, International Judo Federation Sixth Dan*

This is a small book with big ideas. Utilizing his deep understanding and mastery of Judo, Moshe Feldenkrais created a course in practical unarmed self defense for the British during WWII. However, it was in how he addressed his task that we see the mind of a genius at work. Feldenkrais merged age old, Oriental self-defense techniques with the explanatory power of science, combined with his own unique brand of pedagogy to create a novel self defense strategy that is easy to learn and use. Based on the slow and thorough learning of one technique and its applications, the ten lessons artfully disarm the fears and apprehensions of those being trained while giving them the expertise necessary to succeed in combat. For the discerning reader a central idea will become evident: that if one first trains the act to be accomplished from its "ending" it allows for many beginnings. Once an act, here a particular stranglehold, is learned in its simplest form and becomes second nature and can be performed unselfconsciously, then that simple unitary act can be made either more complex or made to fit more complex situations. The approach taken in this book is consonant with the basis of all Feldenkrais' approach to learning. It will be of unquestioned value to both martial artists and *Feldenkrais* practitioners.

Moti Nativ is to be commended not only for bringing this book out of retirement but also for his introduction and commentaries which convey the observations of a true teacher of the martial arts and a *Feldenkrais* Practitioner.

— *Dennis Leri, Feldenkrais Trainer and Martial Artist*

This impactful book reveals a pioneer who is equal parts warrior and educator, and offers a snapshot of a method in the midst of its making.

If you follow the trajectory of training outlined in this book, you'll find the very same strategies and techniques that become the basis of Dr. Feldenkrais' yet-to-be-announced method. By teaching only one martial arts technique, Feldenkrais creates a lesson-like experiment, rich in the interplay of theme and variation. The training reveals the big picture as it clarifies the details and, just as the student begins to put it all together, Moshe changes the action's orientation to space. And so on!

Thank you, Moti, for making this book available once again. The beautiful, user-friendly design is a fitting tribute to its historical importance.

— **Larry Goldfarb,** *Feldenkrais® Trainer*

Both martial artists and movement students will find *Hadaka-Jime The Core Technique for Practical Unarmed Combat* a valuable guide with both practical techniques and profound insights about the learning process. Feldenkrais' clear instructions, peppered with his wry humor and personal philosophy, make this much more than a combat training manual. The illustrations provide a fascinating window into the development of Moshe Feldenkrais' methodology as well as clear instructions to accompany the text.

— **Lavinia Plonka,** Guild Certified *Feldenkrais* Practitioner, author, *What are You Afraid of* and *Walking Your Talk*

# CONTENTS

# FOREWORD

IT is with great awe that I approach the writings of Moshe Feldenkrais. I marvel at the genius of his thought processes and at his fighting spirit. So with great reverence I am writing the foreword to his unique book *Practical Unarmed Combat*.

In this distinctive book, Moshe Feldenkrais lays out a particularly successful training process. His conclusions regarding the essence of learning through clear, direct statements and by implication are clearly presented to the reader. He provides a very detailed and accurate description of specific combat techniques and also presents the reader with principles of the learning process which are valid for all of life's endeavors.

Anyone who reads this book can use it for the practical study of the combat techniques presented or implement the principles to design a personal training program.

## ABOUT MOSHE FELDENKRAIS

Moshe Feldenkrais was born in 1904, in Slavuta, in the present-day Ukrainian Republic. By 1912 his family moved to Baranovich, located in Belarus, Russia. As a fourteen year old boy he undertook a daring journey from his home to the British mandate of Palestine, to lend a hand in building the fledgling Jewish settlement and to play a role in the struggle for an independent Jewish state in the land of Israel. At that time, building the Jewish settlement mainly consisted of hard physical labor, and was often accompanied by violent brawls between the Jewish pioneers and their Arab neighbors. The British governors forbade the pioneers from carrying guns. Even though the pioneers received some self-defense training in Ju-Jitsu, the confrontations often ended in heavy casualties.

Moshe Feldenkrais took an active part in these brawls and came to understand that there were basic flaws in the training that purported to prepare the Jewish warriors to handle these events. He decided to put together his own system of combat. At that time, in addition to his knowledge of Ju-Jitsu, Moshe was well educated in boxing, learning from his friend Amiel (Emil) Avineri[1], also he grabbed whatever he could read and hear, as the American wrestling style "catch as you can", and based on his practical fighting experience he published his first book, *Jiu-Jitsu and Self Defense,* which was designed for Jewish defense forces, the Hagana.[2] Moshe planned to continue his study in France and chose to move shortly before the book's publication in 1931, in part because he was apprehensive about how the British authorities would react to the publication of the book.[3]

While in France he enrolled in an engineering college, the École Spéciale des Travaux Publics de la Ville de Paris.

He subsequently earned his D.Sc. in Physics from the Sorbonne and was a close associate of Nobel Prize Laureate Frederic Joliot-Curie at the Curie Institute in Paris, where they conducted research together.

In France, Moshe continued his involvement with the martial arts. While studying at the École Spéciale des Travaux Publics, he started a ju-jitsu club. Meeting with Professor Jigoro Kano, the founder of Judo, in 1933 was a significant milestone in his development as a martial artist. As a result of this meeting, Moshe developed a strong bond with Judo. Jigoro Kano was impressed by Feldenkrais and was sure that he would rapidly progress towards a perfect possession of Judo. The cooperation between Kano and Feldenkrais made a significant contribution to the development of Judo in France. In 1935 Mikinosuke Kawaishi joined Moshe and also became active in the Club Jiu-Jitsu de France.[4]

Jigoro Kano's influence on the young Feldenkrais was far reaching and, as a result, the phrase 'mind-body' became a permanent feature in Moshe Feldenkrais' vocabulary. Kano's approach to the martial arts resonated with Moshe, and echoes of his philosophy can be found throughout Dr. Feldenkrais' teachings.[5]

In 1940, following the Nazi invasion of France, Moshe fled to England and because of his important knowledge he was posted as scientific officer in the British Admiralty, where he conducted anti-submarine research in Scotland from 1940–1945.

During his stint in the British army, he also taught Judo to the officers and soldiers on his base, which led to the publication of *Practical Unarmed Combat.* After leaving the Admiralty, he was active in the U.K. Budokwai in London, learning from Gunji Koizumi. In 1948, he was involved in founding the European Judo Union and was nominated to serve on its first board.

Moshe Feldenkrais published also three books on Judo that are still used as reliable source material for Judo theory and training. Through the years, the value of Moshe's unique approach to the martial arts was recognized by modern martial arts masters. Gunji Koizumi wrote extensively about the value of Feldenkrais' contribution to Judo.[6]

In 1950 he returned to Israel and was given a senior position in the Science Department of the IDF (Israel Defense Forces). He served in this post until stepping down in 1953 to devote his time and resources to develop and publicize what is known today as the *Feldenkrais Method*®.[7]

## ABOUT *PRACTICAL UNARMED COMBAT*

This book describes an abbreviated training program for soldiers, which in a very short time, gives them the ability to defend themselves against an armed opponent by overpowering him in the most rapid and effective way possible.

The chain of events, which led to the development and implementation of this training program, shows that Moshe Feldenkrais had the courage of his convictions. During World War II, a Home Guard platoon commander participated in a few Judo lessons taught by Moshe, who was also serving in the British army at the time. Subsequently, the commander asked Moshe to train his soldiers in self-defense techniques in the shortest time possible. Moshe jumped at the chance to put into practice an idea that he had been mulling over for a long time – the possibility of developing a fighting method based on one core technique. As Moshe wrote in the preface to *Practical Unarmed Combat*, "I have pointed out elsewhere [in his book, *Judo*] that a self-contained system of defense based on one fundamental movement can easily be evolved."

Moshe Feldenkrais began training one platoon. Another platoon joined the training and eventually the entire battalion completed the course.

Moshe Feldenkrais explains that the course was designed for emergencies and actually called it 'First Aid' for squads that could not engage in long-term training.

Even though he served as a scientist on a base far from the front lines, Moshe understood the advantage enjoyed by a soldier who can confront an enemy in close combat. He contended that the most important issue was training all troops to be as efficient and reliable as possible. In our era, even with state of the art weapons, it is common to teach soldiers methods of unarmed combat.

Following the success of the training course, he wrote *Practical Unarmed Combat* because "it was not practicable to satisfy demands coming from farther and farther away so I compiled this work as a guide for those to whom I cannot give personal attention."[8]

## *PRACTICAL UNARMED COMBAT* IS PRACTICAL

As a martial arts teacher, I have used this book as a resource for developing some of my training programs. I have found that the principles and techniques, which Moshe Feldenkrais posited here, are as relevant now as they were in 1942. It became apparent to me that this book is now virtually unknown by martial arts devotees.

During my research on the thesis the **Synergy of Martial Arts and the *Feldenkrais Method*** [9] I re-read *Practical Unarmed Combat* from the point of view of a *Feldenkrais Method* practitioner. I discovered important principles that, in the past, I had not paid sufficient attention to. Moshe Feldenkrais wrote this book as a martial artist; however his descriptions of martial art techniques and training are weighted with special information that express his knowledge and understanding of the learning process.

This new perception led me to conclude that *Practical Unarmed Combat* is important beyond the field of the martial arts. This book not only provides keystone information for **Feldenkrais Method** practitioners, but will also benefit lay people with its practical approach to life.

Although the book was published during World War II and I assume there are those that will say it is dated, I resolved to publish an expanded edition of *Practical Unarmed Combat* because I believe that the universality of the principles presented here make it a timeless work.

I have chosen to leave the text exactly as Moshe Feldenkrais wrote it, using bold text where he expands on the principles of his approach to learning and movement education. I have also added endnotes to bring into sharper focus some subjects, which Moshe introduced but did not write about in detail because of the minimal structure of the book. I have left it to the wise reader to identify the value of what is written regarding martial arts techniques. In the course of my research, I have unearthed never-published photographs of Moshe taken while he was writing this book. I have taken the liberty of adding them to this new edition.

I hope that in writing this foreword I will succeed in illuminating the uniqueness of this book, emphasizing the important principles found here for the teacher and the trainee.

## DESIGNING THE TRAINING PROGRAM

This book was conceived in the mind (and body) of a man with much experience and knowledge of the martial arts. This man chose, because of the prevailing winds of that era (WWII), to create a system of unarmed combat that focused on one specific technique and, around that technique, to build a suitable training program.

In the foreword of *Practical Unarmed Combat*, Moshe Feldenkrais reveals his thoughts on the course's design.

I would like to emphasize three especially interesting points:

1. **The choice of Judo** - Moshe Feldenkrais argues that Ju-Jitsu had been supplanted by the more efficient Judo[10] and therefore he chose a Judo technique as the basis of the emergency training. As one who educated others about survival and self-defense, Moshe Feldenkrais saw Judo as the source for improving practical combat ability. He explained, "... Judo does not teach so many tricks, but rather inculcates in the mind and body a special sense of balance and action enabling the body to react to an unforeseen attack, smoothly, swiftly, and in the most efficient way."[11]

2. **One technique** - The method presented in *Practical Unarmed Combat* evolves from one core technique. However, a quick look at the text and accompanying photographs tells a different story. Although the trainee is trained to execute one technique with great exactitude, the technique is actually the central junction at which the trainee can arrive from different directions. The trainee learns to implement the technique in a variety of situations and acquires skills that can be applied in a great number of techniques, thus the fighter actually has many options to choose from. Moshe Feldenkrais' unique method of teaching – confining the learning to one technique – paradoxically creates options and options always provide freedom of action.

3. **A thousand repetitions** - Moshe Feldenkrais stressed that the course is designed so that the technique is practiced more than a thousand times, and carried out at the right speed for learning, in order to achieve a high level of skill. He considered true learning successful when the application or performance in the real world conforms to his declaration that "The ultimate value of an exercise lies in the action your body will perform spontaneously, without conscious effort, long after you have forgotten how, when, and where you have learned it."[12] This level of ability to act is the goal of martial arts, being able to react to any threat efficiently and effectively with no preparation. Dr. Masaaki

Hatsumi describes this state of mind as "Being Zero" when confronting an attacker.[13]

## THE CORE TECHNIQUE IS THE CORE PRINCIPLE

Moshe Feldenkrais chose Hadaka-Jime,[14] or the naked arm strangulation technique, as the core technique. He had written extensively about this strangulation technique in his book *Judo – The Art of Defense and Attack* (1941) maintaining that the stranglehold itself is useful for defending oneself against attacks, in which the attacker thrusts his hands forward toward his victim.

Even at the beginning of his journey as a martial artist, Moshe Feldenkrais was mindful of the effectiveness and the power of strangulation. In his first book, *Jiu-Jitsu and Self Defense* (1931) he demonstrated the use of the strangulation technique from the rear as a way to overpower and neutralize an opponent (Fig. a). He took care to warn the reader of the danger involved in performing this technique in an uncontrolled manner. During the years he was active in the Jiu-Jitsu Club de France he further explored this technique (Fig. b) and wrote about it in his book *ABC du Judo* (1938) (Fig. c).

The strangulation technique is familiar to millions of people all over the world, but to the best of my knowledge Moshe Feldenkrais is the only one who chose it as the cornerstone of a quick training program designed for combat troops. Even those

Fig. a: *From Moshe's Hebrew book, Jiu-Jitsu and Self Defense, published in 1931 for the Haganah*

Fig. b: *From the Jiu-jitsu Club in France*

who might have reservations regarding the choice of this particular technique will recognize that the process of acquiring this tactic includes a wide spectrum of learning that brings the fighter to the most effective performance. Accepting this point of view, it becomes obvious that the specific technique becomes secondary to the more important learning process. It must be emphasized that this principle can be applied to all fields of endeavor, whether training for practical combat or any other urgent training. Catching on to the basic principle allows the student to construct a similar program for achieving goals in his or her particular field.

## FIRST LEARN TO KILL AND THEN LEARN TO HUNT

Fig. c: *From* A.B.C. du Judo

One of Moshe Feldenkrais' basic precepts regarding learning was that one must first acquire the ability, and then put it to practical use. This concept is basic to *Practical Unarmed Combat*. Lessons one through three teach the core technique, by demonstrating detailed body manipulation, and showing its use in various situations. Once the technique has been mastered, Feldenkrais says "if you feel that the weapon kills and that you can depend on it, you can proceed to learn something about hunting." Starting with lesson four, the trainee is taught practical application of the core technique.

So, how do you learn to hunt? Speed, repetition, timing, and a relaxed attitude.

Perusing Moshe Feldenkrais' text, we can glean important insights into how he approached improving the learning process. For instance: "Another very important thing to observe is the nonchalant and relaxed attitude. The motion should not stiffen your legs and hips. Relaxation comes of course with skill, but if you think [are aware] of it, you will acquire it sooner."[15]

We also find a significant statement concerning the basis of movement education: "You must therefore proceed cautiously from the start, sacrificing speed to precision, so that the spontaneous movement on which you depend will be the correct one – there being the correct mental picture only in your unconscious memory."[16]

It is interesting to note that the idea of taking the time one needs to learn seems contradictory when considered in the context of the minimal framework of a ten hour course. Feldenkrais' intent was to achieve true learning even in an urgent course demanding quick results. He warned that "haste creates confusion" and urged his students not to confound speed with haste. He claimed that it is impossible to achieve rapid improvement when attempting to execute the action too fast. Distinguishing between rapid and organized action, as opposed to hasty action performed without awareness, and the understanding produced by recognizing the difference was a basic issue for Moshe when he considered the learning process.[17]

## PRACTICAL APPLICATIONS

Over a decade ago, during my training as a *Feldenkrais Method* practitioner, I happened upon *Practical Unarmed Combat* while browsing the Feldenkrais Institute library in Tel Aviv. The timing was fortuitous as the book fell into my hands at a time when I had just completed a project in which, working with a hand-picked group, I researched practical techniques for overpowering opponents for specific missions. The experiments and exercises I used during the project led me to conclude that strangulation from the rear is the most effective means of rapidly overpowering an armed opponent. I was amazed to discover that this exact solution had already been offered by Moshe Feldenkrais many years ago. I was sorry that I had not discovered this book at the beginning of the project because it would have been a great help and would have saved me a lot of time. Since then I have, on many occasions, used the training process exactly as described by Moshe Feldenkrais in this book. I also found that paying close attention to his remarks on the learning process made it possible for me to implement this training in heterogeneous groups.

Recently, during the research I have undertaken concerning the **Synergy of Martial Arts and the *Feldenkrais Method,*** I was pleased to discover that Moshe Feldenkrais' concept of core technique was put to practical use. Shortly after the publication of *Practical Unarmed Combat*, the book found its way into the hands of the team responsible for designing KAPAP (Face-to-Face Combat), as a new training method for the Haganah. The KAPAP was famous for its stick fighting techniques, combined with other fighting skills.[18] Maishel (Moshe) Horowitz, who led the team, told me that he used the concept of one specific technique for emergency training. He added that he was once given just twenty-four hours to prepare fighters for combat and trained them concentrating on one technique. The training proved successful and the results on the battlefield were excellent. Maishel told me that he regrets that he had not discovered the book earlier, which was exactly how I felt.

## PRACTICAL LEARNING

The essence of Dr. Feldenkrais' thought is the principles and mechanisms of learning, which can be applied in all situations and are not limited to any particular field. The process of learning is a theme throughout all his work, coming to full fruition in the *Feldenkrais Method*.

During the writing of *Practical Unarmed Combat*, Moshe Feldenkrais had already begun to formulate the series of lectures that he gave during 1943-1944 for the Association of Scientific Workers in Fairlie, Scotland.[19] One of the topics he presented was "Learning - The Uniqueness of Man". He emphasized the difficulties in learning new responses, "The acquisition of a new response is made possible only by the extinction of the inborn responses. It is not impossible but extremely laborious." He surmounted the difficulties in this unique training.

Moshe proved that everyone can learn. It is significant that he used the principles presented in *Practical Unarmed Combat* to train Home Guard soldiers, who were certainly not elite combat troops.

He believed that creating an environment conducive to learning is not less important than the instruction itself.

Careful reading of *Practical Unarmed Combat* reveals that Moshe Feldenkrais was not concerned only with technique. He covers diverse subjects that are relevant to training and combat environments, such as: how to apply the technique when opponents are physically mismatched, awareness of more than one opponent, how to counter resistance, the training surface, safety issues, and more.

There are also hints of how to be more effective during the interaction with the attacker. For example, when describing how to counter a knife or bayonet attack, he says, "Keep your eyes open, following the opponent's elbow."[20] Or, "Pay attention to your left hand gripping the rifle...it makes the weapon as much yours as his."[21]

His user-friendly approach to learning is reflected in the nuggets of humor found throughout the book. For example, when talking about practicing the technique with a partner he says, "A quarter of your strength should be enough to make your opponent tap [surrender]. The other three quarters should be kept in reserve for an extremely powerful opponent or to make good any imperfection in performance in case of emergency, otherwise, if you are not careful you will have to look for another victim for your further study." Another example of his great intuition regarding how humans learn can be found in the statement, "Repeat as many times as you can before becoming bored with it... ."[22] Moshe uses a Samurai tale to demonstrate the significance of correct timing and to illustrate the concept of choosing the right timing to overcome an attacker.[23] The use of the story is unusual in a book focused on practical combat, but it foreshadows the teaching techniques of a later period when he taught the *Feldenkrais Method*.

Feldenkrais drew on his extensive scientific knowledge, as evidenced by the drawings he added to illustrate the correct execution of the stranglehold.[24] It is interesting to note that his explanation of the Hadaka-Jime technique was unique and cannot be found in any Judo books from that time.

Moshe Feldenkrais cautions readers that, more than simply reading the material, actual experience and practice of the technique is necessary to learn it. As Miyamoto Musashi, the author of *The Book of Five Rings,* wrote, "Who in this world can obtain my correct Way of the martial arts? Whoever would get to the heart of it, let him do so with conviction, practicing in the morning and training in the evening. After he has polished his techniques and gained independent freedom of movement, he will naturally gain miraculous powers, and his free and easy strength will be wonderful."

## CONCLUSION

The course that Moshe Feldenkrais constructed is comprised of ten lessons, one hour each, so the entire course is only ten hours long. I would like to point out that the use of the term 'lesson', and not the usual term 'training', already hints at Moshe Feldenkrais' approach that is aimed at education and learning. The results prove the effectiveness of the approach. Moshe Feldenkrais succeeded in training troops using the method described in his book.

This book, which ostensibly deals with just one technique, offers an efficient methodology for all training and instruction. My own experience has convinced me that this path is superior when working with experienced martial artists and with those inexperienced in the techniques of hand to hand combat. Moreover, the technique that Moshe Feldenkrais chose, strangulation from the rear, is most efficient.

*Practical Unarmed Combat* can be used in many ways: you can use the book to learn or teach the same practical self defense training/course, you can use the concept and information to construct your own "first aid" self defense technique, and you can apply its principles to all fields where learning and mastery result in achieving the maximum.

# PREFACE

**I HAVE** often been asked, after Judo contests or demonstrations, to show a "trick" by which one can invariably master an opponent. These requests were put in a way that left no doubt that their authors were convinced that such a thing would be too good to be true.

Yet this is not quite impossible and there are "tricks," the application of which is very general. I have pointed out elsewhere[25] that a self-contained system of defence based "on one fundamental movement can easily be evolved." This book presents one such system based on a simple movement which can be learned by everybody: men and women, old and young, for it demands no special feats of strength, swiftness or general fitness. Its effect is immediate after a few trials and the only thing to learn is how to get the chance of securing the hold. That is what this book is out to teach you.

Quite recently, after attending a few Judo lessons under my instruction, Lieutenant Felix G. Apthorpe commanding a Home Guard platoon approached me with the request to teach his men unarmed combat.

This gave me the opportunity of testing in practice the soundness of the idea underlying this work. The result was encouraging. After a few lessons another platoon in the vicinity joined in. In a few months practically the whole battalion has been trained. This was due to the tenacity and devotion of Mr. Caldwell Ker. His clear understanding and helpfulness turned hard work into real pleasure.

It was not practicable to satisfy demands coming from farther and farther away so I compiled this work as a guide for those to whom I cannot give personal attention.

I am glad to express my thanks to Lieutenant Apthorpe and to Lieutenant T. W. Hirst whose keenness in securing any possible advantage for their men gave me the possibility of perfecting this work.

My thanks are also due to Sergeant R. D. Keynes and Corporal Hughes who kindly agreed to figure in the illustrations and to Mr. Donald S. Herbert, F.R.P.S., for his kindness and skill in preparing the photographs.

The text has greatly benefited as a result of critical reading by my friends, G. N. Ward and Dr. H. F. Willis, and I am indebted to Miss Madge King for the careful preparation of the typescript.

# INTRODUCTION

*Concepts of the Practical Unarmed Combat Training*

**IT** goes without saying that without "tools" nobody can fight a soldier armed with modern weapons with any chance of success when attacked from a distance. We naturally assume then that you are provided with adequate "tools" to meet the enemy at least on equal terms.

There are, however, many valid reasons why you should acquire a sufficient amount of skill in using your body only for your defence. You cannot carry with you all the ammunition you may want. You may be surprised at close quarters by the attacker so that you cannot make use of your weapons.

You may be forced by a superior enemy to surrender your arms, and so on. A glance through the illustrations will convince you that there are situations in which only a man in the forces is likely to be involved and from which he cannot extricate himself without a weapon unless he uses the methods depicted.

It is universally admitted today that a man of the forces conversant with unarmed combat is a greater asset than one who is not. The actual number of lives saved in modern warfare by unarmed combat methods may as yet be very insignificant. There is, however, much likelihood that it will be greater than is commonly believed before this war is over.

But this point is irrelevant and unimportant compared with the major issue of rendering the whole of the fighting forces more efficient and reliable. That it is so, is borne out by the inclusion of unarmed combat methods in the training of picked troops like the Commandos.

When considering means of defence against an armed opponent it is natural to think of Ju-Jitsu, as indeed it is the only method of dealing with this subject. (It may be interesting to notice, by the way, that the word Ju-Jitsu is used only in Europe and is obsolete in the country in which it originated, as is the method it is used to denote. Both are replaced by a more scientific and much more efficient system called Judo).

Anyone who has tried to acquire a knowledge of this art has certainly soon become aware of the considerable time that has to be devoted to the acquisition of the skill necessary for successful application of the method. Any Judo expert will tell you that something like five years of two lessons a week are necessary in order to become reasonably conversant with all the ways of this subtle art.

For Judo does not teach so many tricks, but rather **inculcates in the mind and body a special sense of balance and action** enabling the body to react to an unforeseen attack, smoothly, swiftly and in the most efficient way.

Even if we decided only upon a limited number of tricks, at least a few months would be required, for indeed the whole time is wasted if the men do not feel more confident than before, and they will not feel confident unless a high degree of skill is attained. Without this the acquired knowledge is of little practical avail, if any. Thus, long and meticulous training cannot be dispensed with even in such a scheme.

From the point of view of the Home Guard here and elsewhere, we cannot launch ourselves on a long term training. **It has to be made ready for an emergency, which may take place while you are reading these lines. That is why I devised this emergency course. It provides "first-aid" equipment.** Good medical treatment will be looked for as soon as possible. If we have the leisure to build up subsequently all-round fighters out of all the men, so much the better. But a "first-aid " is always a good acquisition.

Now let us see what our first-aid box contains and whether we can depend on it in case of emergency.

**A hasty glance through the text and illustrations in the book will show you that the field covered is quite large. At any rate the most probable cases of emergency are met. It will also show you that it is all centered around one fundamental movement.**

The advantages of such a condensed system are very substantial for, in a lesson lasting one hour, a single movement can be repeated at least a hundred times; then in the following lessons this movement appears repeatedly in unexpected modes and applications through which a keen interest is maintained during the entire course. **By the time this is completed one has repeated the fundamental movement more than a thousand times, which is sufficient to attain a high degree of skill in its performance.**

**There being only one movement which is so familiar that little conscious effort is necessary to bring it instantaneously into action.** There is, moreover, no room left for making mistakes as to the choice of an appropriate movement.

The great advantage, however, lies in the fact that in a fortnight or so, the whole body of a service, the Home Guard or others could be trained and made ready for an emergency which may be imminent.

No special athletic feats, or excessive strength, are required for the successful execution of the movement. This makes it especially suitable for the Home Guard where all ages are represented. In the hands of virile young men it will be a very dangerous weapon.

Incidentally it may be interesting to notice that the movement in question is of little avail against a man wearing a British tin hat. The horizontal rim projecting backwards is a real hindrance to its performance, while the enemy, as can be ascertained from "Spot at Sight Chart No. 1" adopted a tin hat that makes the application of the movement easier and more effective.

But all this is only the background for the outstanding feature of the movement, namely, its efficiency. It is easy to secure, it works against a much stronger opponent as well as against a weak one; moreover you are in safety while applying it. In short you can depend on it. All that is necessary is the will to learn it and to try at once.

# WARNING
## *Safety Advice*

**HURRY creates confusion. Very little speed is gained by trying to go too fast. Real speed is gained by simple, smooth, and well balanced movements.** The only way of acquiring these is repetition - calm repetition - especially in the beginning before you are absolutely sure that you have well assimilated the text.

You must not use your full strength. This would be sufficient to kill your opponent, and therefore cannot be tried twice on the same man. **If you cannot obtain submission with little effort your execution is incorrect.** The most common mistakes are pointed out and great care has been taken to make things clear. Read the particular passage again before applying more strength.

The Judo method of announcing submission or "breaking" an engagement should be adopted. That is, when your opponent taps on his thigh, on the floor or on your body with his hand, or just claps one hand against the other, you should invariably and instantly relax and set him free, otherwise permanent injury is unavoidable. The tapping should consist of two successive loud reports produced by the hand at the points of contact mentioned above.

All jerks should be avoided. Increase your effort gradually until your opponent taps. After a few trials you will feel how far you can go without injuring him and will get the knack of acting smoothly and swiftly without jerks. Jerky movements are often harmful but never reliably efficient, while skillfully controlled movements can be as deadly as necessary.

The other extreme, i.e., unnecessary softness in execution, is also to be avoided. You should secure the proper hold and carry it out firmly until your opponent taps. Don't forget that one day your life may depend on that hold and you should be able to bring your movement to its ultimate conclusion.

The movements throughout the book are simple; indeed they are so simple that a special warning is necessary. Many will be prone to think that reading or trying them once or twice would do. On the other hand some may think they are too simple to be of any use. Well, the most marvelous music is played by simple finger touches on a simple key of a piano.

It becomes marvelous when these movements are done by a master. **Doing the right thing at the right moment, with ease and the skill acquired by constant exercise, enables the man to convey the most delicate feeling just by simple touches.** You can see and hear how it is done but you can hardly hope to produce the same effect. Without work no genius is of any avail. Repeat the movements as often as instructed, as closely as you can, and you will soon realize that you have not been wasting your time.

## WARNING

The illustrations show action with bare weapons. To begin with, you must use a wooden stick of the size of a knife, with rounded edges, or use the bayonet in its scabbard.

Only after your movements become natural, simple and smooth should you attempt to use naked steel. When you do, you must repeat the movements in slow motion only, until you get used to the sight of the glittering weapon.

However proficient and sure of yourself you may feel, you might slip, your opponent may prod the weapon forward just when you were about to say something and the damage is done. So again, be careful! At the same time don't think that training with harmless weapons will do. **Unless used to the sight of steel pointing at you, exceptional qualities are necessary to enable you to keep your head in real action.**

# FIRST LESSON
*The Core Technique, Basic Application*

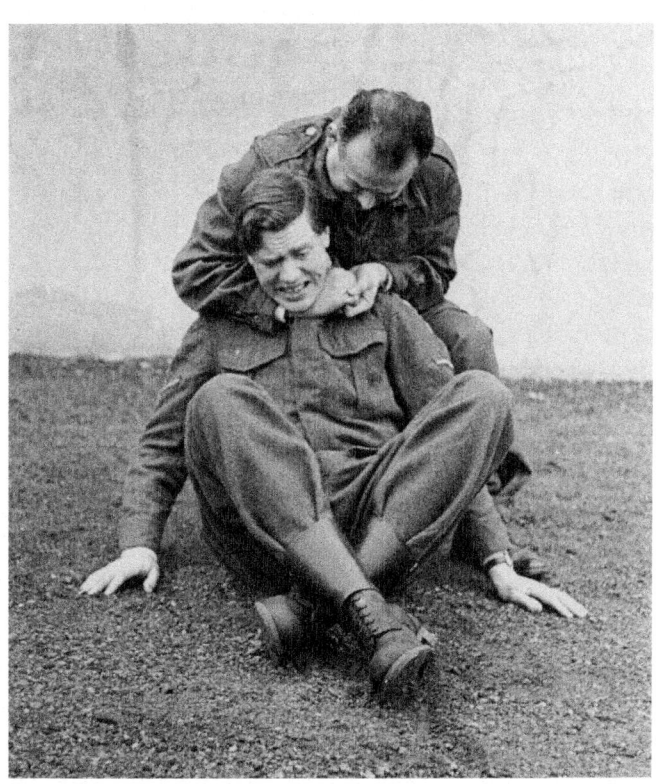

**THE** ultimate value of an exercise lies in the action your body will perform spontaneously, without conscious effort, long after you have forgotten how, when and where you have learned it. The operation you have exercised repeatedly, rather than what you had in mind, is voluntarily executed by the physical body and is readily reproduced in spite of yourself.

It is important to realise this before you start training, for your life may one day depend on how well you were trained.

If from the beginning you perform alternately correct and faulty movements your body will have a tendency to reproduce either of them. You must therefore proceed cautiously from the start, sacrificing speed to precision, so that the spontaneous movement on which you depend will be the correct one—there being the correct mental picture only in your unconscious memory. It is more profitable to do a movement ten times correctly, than a hundred times where faulty and correct movement alternate at random.

Now let your opponent sit on the floor in the position shown in Fig. 1. Kneel on your right knee close behind him. Put your right forearm round his neck, clasp your hands together and gradually, without jerks, tighten your grip until he taps on his thigh. Repeat three times and change places with your opponent.

Resume your position behind the sitting opponent as before. Bring your right forearm round his neck and turn your

Fig. 1          Fig. 2

right wrist anticlockwise as if unscrewing a screw then slide it in this twisted position under his chin. Clasp your hand as shown in Fig. 2. Tighten your grip until he taps.

Note the way the hands are kept ready in Fig. 1 as well as the position of the left forearm placed on the opponent's shoulder. It is also essential that the left hand should face palm upwards and be under the right and not vice versa.

The details of the two last paragraphs are of paramount importance for they transform the simple tightening of your arm into a complex movement which, in addition to the compression of the throat, exerts a constriction of the wind-pipe (trachea) and a pull upwards. The action of your right forearm untwisting itself back to its normal position is similar to that of the wheel in Fig. 3 and the effect on the windpipe (trachea) is

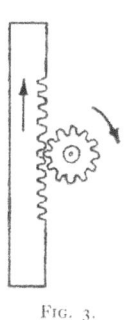

Fɪɢ. 3.

Fig. 3

Fig. 4

Fig. 5

the same as on the rack, plus a compression.

The relative position of your hands makes sure that the narrowest and hardest part of your right forearm is in contact with the opponent's throat, thus applying the maximum possible pressure.

Examine Fig. 2 attentively and note the position of the right arm behind the nape of the opponent. Beginners often press their chest bone against the opponent's nape. This is wrong and it is ineffective.

Make sure you have grasped correctly what you are expected to do; try six times and let your opponent go through the same number of movements.

Fig. 4 shows the movement completed. The tightening of the arms is accompanied by a push of the right arm, or rather the shoulder, against the nape and a hardly noticeable shift of your hands to your left, your forearm thus sawing his throat. Note the opponent's position. His balance is slightly broken backwards. You are now not only choking him but pulling the vertebrae of his neck powerfully apart.

Be careful not to be brisk and jerky but to use only a small part of your strength, for the dislocation of these vertebrae, or the head, may be fatal and even a slight sprain may produce incurable paralysis of the limbs and trunk.

Repeat the movement again, paying due attention to all the details.

Resume the position of Fig. 4. Lift your right knee off the ground, step back one pace without letting go the opponent's head, and break his balance completely. His belt should now be touching the ground. Fig. 5 shows this position. He is no longer sitting, but is lying on his back with his legs in the air. The weight of his body is now added to increase the stress on the vertebrae of the nape of the neck.

Study the position of your head in Figs. 5, 13 and 16, and that of your right shoulder in Figs. 26 and 27 if the opponent's head continues to slip out of your hold.

Note how wide apart your feet should be. This gives you a very stable lateral balance which enables you to check any wriggling or lateral twist of a powerful opponent fighting for his life. This is important only during the very short instant of breaking the opponent's balance – afterwards the hold tells instantly, as the slightest effort of your arms and the right shoulder will silence the opponent for good.

Remembering this, do not use too much strength while training. Repeat a dozen times and let your opponent do the same.

# SECOND LESSON
*The Core Technique, Completions*

Fig. 2

Fig. 6

Fig. 7

Fig. 8

**TAKE** up the position of Fig. 2, kneeling on your right knee behind the opponent. Bend your head forward so that your right cheek touches his left cheek, get up to your feet (Fig. 6) and roll backwards straight on to your back. You must avoid sitting down and then rolling on your back as this is much slower and moreover, makes the unpleasant contact of the base of the spine (coccyx) with the ground, unavoidable.

While rolling on to your back wrap your legs around the opponent, just above his hips, where he wears his belt, and hook them as shown in Fig. 7. Roll over to your left side, take the upper part of your body right backwards, and tighten your arms, at the same time pushing your opponent forward with your hips as in Fig. 8. The result is obvious.

Fig. 8a

Again remember to proceed smoothly without jerks and using only a fraction of your full strength. **A quarter of your strength should be enough to make your opponent tap. The other three quarters should be kept in reserve for an extremely powerful opponent or to make good any imperfection in performance in case of emergency, otherwise, if you are not careful you will have to look for another victim for your further study.**

You can of course roll over to your right and continue as before. This is shown in Fig. 8a. You will soon learn to use these backward rolls.

Fig. 9          Fig. 10          Fig. 11          Fig. 12          Fig. 13

Now both stand upright. Face your opponent's back (Fig. 9), slide your right arm with your wrist turned anticlockwise as clearly seen in the figure. Clasp your hands in the usual way, carefully observing all the details, especially that of the pressure produced by your left forearm on the opponent's left shoulder. Tighten your arms, and when sufficient pressure is exerted by your right forearm, untwist (Fig. 10) your right wrist to its normal position. As explained in Fig. 3, your forearm will engage like a cog under the chin to the correct position.

Pull the opponent's head backwards to lean against your right shoulder, pushing forward powerfully (there is no danger this time), with your hips as in Fig. 11. Note also the use of the right knee in the figure.

Fig. 9 has been made on purpose to show how to deal with an opponent who has become aware of your attack and has lowered his chin, preventing you from sliding your forearm to the required position. This will, of course, not be the general case, but if you get the habit of twisting your right wrist every time you wrap your arm around the opponent you will find no difficulty in carrying out your movement even if the opponent has lowered his chin as described.

Fig. 14

The opponent's balance having been broken, move backwards as in Fig. 12, tugging down, and at the same time improving your own balance by spreading your legs apart as in Fig. 13. Move backwards until the opponent's belt touches the ground and then push forward with your shoulder, tightening your arms with the effect shown in Fig. 14.

Repeat, starting from the standing position as above, a dozen times at least, until all the details are fused into a single smooth movement, and then let your opponent do the same.

Fig. 15                    Fig. 16

If the opponent tries to get hold of you as in Fig. 15 (which is the only thing he can do), take no notice of him. Tug down (see illustration) and resume the position of the body shown in Fig. 16, where the whole weight of your body and the strength of your loins are brought into play. Be careful and smooth in your movements while trying. Repeat several times.

Note the way the opponent is pinned to the ground in Fig. 16. Constant pressure against his throat must be maintained with the arm, otherwise you will be helping him to sit up and all the pains taken will be wasted.

The movements shown in Figs. 5, 14 and 16 show the climax to which all our efforts tend. Repeat it twenty times, and more if necessary, until you get the knack of compelling the opponent, without hesitation or failure, to submit and tap. In real action you would go on until all resistance is blotted out.

Let us examine what your opponent could do to prevent you from achieving this. We have already dealt with him when he is pressing the chin down, and the movement is carried out with no difficulty in spite of it.

Fig. 17         Fig. 18

He may try to push you back as in Fig. 17 and make you lose your balance. Here the movement that we have learned in the beginning of this lesson comes in. If you feel him attempting such an action, yield to it, roll straight on your back (Fig. 18) and finish as usual.

Fig. 19        Fig. 20        Fig. 21        Fig. 22

He could also catch your right forearm as shown in Fig. 19, thus making it impossible to produce any compression of the throat and push you backwards, at the same time bringing his other hand to help the first as in Fig. 20. Again yield to his impetus, roll on your back, wrap your legs around him but do not hook them. Fig. 21 shows how the legs are wrapped around his thighs this time. Turn to your right side or left side as shown in Fig. 22, push your groins as far forward as you can (without jerking, of course, while training), your legs holding his thigh backwards, and now tug powerfully but gradually further backwards, straightening your back, while holding him tightly with your arms close to your chest. He cannot make the usual sign of submission, for if he lets go with his hands a sudden increase of flexion of his body will break the small of his backbone.

The same result will be achieved if you jerk or use your full strength. So be careful and let him free as soon as he grunts for this is the only thing he can do in his present predicament. Fig. 23 shows the opponent having succeeded in preventing your right arm from touching his throat. It is obvious from the illustration that this will not help him to get free.

You may be tempted to finish the movement always with a roll on your back; indeed it is easier than the finish we have learned before and which is shown in Figs. 5, 14 or 16.

**Nevertheless you must train yourself to proceed generally as we have learned originally, as this gives you greater freedom and can be performed with lightning rapidity.**

Fig. 23

Moreover, as soon as you hear the ominous crack of the victim's neck, you are free and ready to face other opponents.

You can also just bring the opponent on to his back, then kick in the region of his ear and you are again ready to fight other enemies.

Rolling on your back entangles you for somewhat longer, during which time you are helpless should a third person intervene. Learn it properly but use it only when compelled to, i.e., only if through your slowness or for any other reason your opponent succeeds in getting hold of your forearm or in pushing you off your balance, as previously explained.

# THIRD LESSON

*The Core Technique, Silent Attack from the Rear*

Fig. 24

Fig. 25

Fig. 26

Fig. 27

**YOU** may derive encouragement by realising that after two lessons only, you could deal with a sentry, for instance, much better than if you were armed. If you succeeded in approaching him within leaping distance (Fig. 24) you have a better chance of success in overcoming your opponent than by shooting a pistol or using cold steel. The first makes noise; the second does not prevent him from making a noise.

Fig. 24 also shows what to do if you are short and your opponent tall. Take up the position of the shorter man in the figure, leap on to the opponent's back, throwing your right forearm under his chin and clasping your hands as usual. (See. Fig. 2).

Note the position of your feet in Fig. 25. You should squeeze your opponent with your knees only, but beware of throwing your legs around his waist. It is most likely, indeed, that they will be grabbed and held tightly, and unless your lock tells instantly the opponent can throw himself on to his back, and the base of your spine (coccyx) will bear the brunt of the impact against the ground under the double weight.

If, on the other hand you follow the illustration closely, you will see that your feet can be put on the ground if necessary. In fact this should be done simultaneously with the clasping of your hands. Weighing down, while your knees push forward and downwards, breaks his balance; then proceed as in Fig. 26. This is your customary movement and Fig. 27 shows the usual result. Repeat ten or twenty times and change places with your opponent.

Fig. 28

Fig. 29

Fig. 30

Fig. 31

Again, if you are very small compared with your opponent, you may, though it is very unlikely, find yourself hurled forward over your opponent's shoulder as in Fig. 28. Cling to him, squeezing your knees together as hard as you can and strangle as much as you can.

On feeling your opponent stooping forward, bring your feet inside his thighs as in Fig. 29. The illustration shows the position which your opponent is most likely to assume under the momentum of the two bodies hurled forward.

Round your shoulders and tuck your head down and you will find yourself rolling over as in Fig. 30. After all the trouble taken by your opponent you are in the most favourable position you could have wished for, as shown in Fig. 31.

You will notice that the completion of this movement is the same as that in Fig. 8, on page 23.

Though the photographs were taken on concrete, you should make your first attempts on a soft lawn several times, before attempting it on a hard floor. Repeat as many times as you can and let your opponent do the same. With a little training you will find it easy to make your opponent roll to the side instead of rolling straight overhead. Little imagination is necessary to see this on a close inspection of Fig. 29.

**The reader who is indulging in perusal only, without practical application, is now invited to stop and give it a trial. Things look so complex when described in words and on paper. They are so much simpler to do, and to understand**

**by the experience of the physical body.** Follow the instructions of this book or those of a better one. Neither are worth reading if they cannot convince you to start practicing at once.

The first phase of our study is now complete. It is as if you had acquired a weapon and learned how it functions.

You have also learned how to handle it so that it does not misfire. **If you feel that the weapon kills and that you can depend on it, you can proceed to learn something about hunting, for you need more than a good gun to become a skilled hunter.** If you don't feel that way, continue practicing until you are convinced in your own mind that you can master any opponent, providing you can approach close enough from behind.

# FOURTH LESSON

*Moving Behind the Attacker, Defense Against Knife Stab to the Neck*

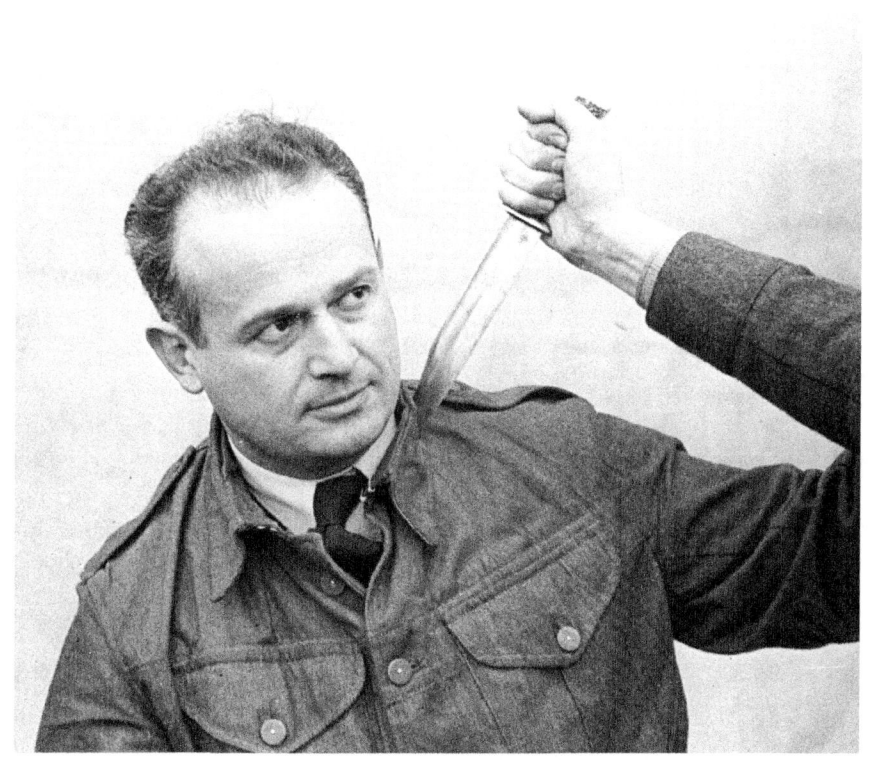

Fig. 32      Fig. 33      Fig. 33b      Fig.33c      Fig. 34

**STAND** right in front of your opponent, facing him. Reach out your left hand, get hold of his right sleeve half way between his wrist and his elbow, at the same time stepping forward and slightly to your left with your left foot. Fig. 32 shows this accomplished.

Try the hold again, this time with a short pull on the grabbed sleeve towards your right and a larger step with your left foot behind the opponent, just skimming his body.

Start again, making sure you let go the sleeve at the end of your short pull to the right and lifting your right arm bent at right angles at the elbow. Fig. 33, naturally leading to Fig. 34, shows this in action. Clasp your hands as usual, your left forearm carefully placed on his shoulder in the way already learnt.

Tighten your arms, pushing forward with your groins and you have learned how to secure the lock on a man who attacks facing you.

This short pull (Fig. 32) is not meant to be strong enough to pull the opponent forward. He may be so much heavier and stronger than yourself that it is impossible for you to achieve this. Moreover, this is not looked for. A man pulled in this way will always stiffen his body to resist. It is only meant to make sure that during the short interval while you are shifting your body on to your left foot (Fig. 33) your opponent is engaged in resisting your pull, i.e., he is not doing anything to interfere with your securing the advantageous position behind him.

If you bend and lift your right arm just when you shift your

Fig. 34a                    Fig. 34b

body on to your left foot, there is no great harm in pulling the sleeve hard. But too hard a pull will spoil everything. The right one is the pull that is just sufficient to make him step forward with his right leg as shown in Fig. 33.

**Another very important thing to observe is the nonchalant and relaxed attitude (Fig. 32). The motion should not stiffen your legs and hips. Relaxation comes of course with skill, but if you think of it you will acquire it sooner.**

Now try twenty times at least and change places with your opponent. The more you do this movement the better. Repeat it until the pull on the sleeve ends with the opponent in the position of tapping in one smooth single stroke, and then try again.

The same movement is now to be repeated, pulling the opponent's left sleeve with your right hand. Now step forward with your right foot and slightly to your right while pulling the sleeve with a short soft motion, at the end of which you loose the sleeve. Bring your right hand around the opponent's neck and conclude as usual. You must not invert the position of your hands in the final lock, irrespective of whether the hold is applied after shifting yourself into position, either from the right or the left of the opponent.

There should be only one way to finish off the hold. If you learn both holds you leave room for confusion at the most critical moment. **Some people have a mania for symmetry in the movements of their body. They must know that perfect**

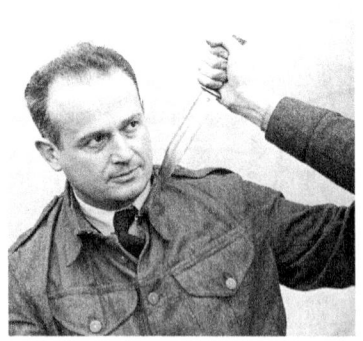

Fig. 35

Fig. 36

Fig. 37

Fig. 38

**symmetry is almost excluded and in our case futile, and endangers the soundness of the whole edifice.**

You can hardly imagine an attack by an armed or unarmed adversary without his arm more or less thrust forward. Any such attack is liable to be thwarted and turned to your advantage by the methods you have learned. We shall go through the most dangerous ones and the less obvious.

Suppose your opponent is about to stab you. He may go for your throat, or more generally, for the upper part of your trunk, in which case he will be holding the knife and aiming in the manner shown in Fig. 35.

This is a very dangerous attack, for the slightest penetration of the weapon will sever vital organs like the common carotid or jugular vein or, if the blade is wide, both at once. A deeper penetration will cut through the bronchus.

To the disappointment of those who believe nature to have taken the greatest care of man it is quite obvious that no protection is provided for this part of the body. Unless we use the whole of the body to destroy our assailant nothing will stand between us as a mechanical shield. In fact any animal or beast attacking a man goes primarily straight for his throat with its fangs.

Let your opponent take a smooth stick with rounded ends and use it as a knife. At this stage to use a real knife will be looking for trouble and you may be sure you will get it. So stick to the stick.

Fig. 36 shows the relative positions to be taken up. Let your

Fig. 39          Fig. 40          Fig. 41          Fig. 42

opponent proceed in slow motion, moving his stick towards your throat. With your left hand, the thumb being kept flat along the palm as seen in Figs. 37 and 38, push over his arm towards your right. This push should be a brisk, short sweep. Your hand should touch the opponent's arm just above his elbow, if his arm is somewhat bent at the elbow (Fig. 37), or at the elbow if the arm is more or less straight as in Fig. 38.

Step with your left foot forward and to your left, at the same time lowering your body by bending the knees. Fig. 38 is very instructive in this respect. Keep your eyes open, following the opponent's elbow. Note how far the steel is kept away from you in correct execution. Even a bayonet would not be long enough to touch you. This is where our method is so much safer than some used elsewhere.

The push over to your right is not meant to turn your opponent, though in swift action it sometimes does. It should only clear the way for you to move behind the opponent as already explained in conjunction with Fig. 33.

It is obvious that the thrust being deviated and avoided, the usual fate awaits your assailant, and Figs. 39-42 are self-explanatory.

Repeat slowly ten times, and after your opponent has done the same try a little faster. Try to be simple, smooth and precise in your movement. **No haste or use of strength will make your movement more efficient, but calm repetition will.**

So repeat as many times as you can before becoming bored with it and change positions as customary.

# FIFTH LESSON

*Defense Against Knife Stab to Abdomen, and Against Alternate Attacks*

Fig. 43　　　　　　　　　　Fig. 44　　　　　　　　　　Fig. 45

**GO** through the last lesson rapidly.

Now let your opponent attack you with his wooden knife as in Fig. 43. Note the point of the knife thrusting upwards. A simple thrust forward is very likely to hit the belt, cartridges or other objects that will stop the knife from producing a deadly wound.

Stand exactly in front of your attacker, hardly lifting your heels from the ground, your hands hanging relaxed. Let him thrust his weapon, aiming at your abdomen. Step with your left foot to your left and slightly forward, while your left hand pushes the attacking arm (behind the elbow) over to your right with a short, smooth and quick movement.

Examine Fig. 44 and note the stooping attitude of the body

which is due to the man withdrawing his abdomen away from the point of the knife. Keeping slightly on your tip-toes facilitates this attitude. Note also the position of the thumb held tightly alongside the other fingers, the hand being held flat.

Start the movement afresh, another thrust being directed at your abdomen. Your sharp push of the opponent's elbow to your right is now accompanied by a smart step to your left bringing you behind him as usual. Fig. 45 shows this clearly.

Beginners often keep up the pressure with the left hand against the opponent's elbow too long. This should be avoided, for once the knife is deviated, following up the elbow serves no purpose. Moreover, it hinders your movement forward and delays your left hand clasping your right hand. This figure also

Fig. 46

Fig. 47

Fig. 48

shows your right arm already bent and sliding under the opponent's chin before he has realized what is happening.

**Note that you need not hurry. Your movement is swift because you are doing the right thing without wasting your time, useless agitation being eliminated by the clear knowledge of what you are doing.**

Fig. 46 shows another view of the position depicted in Fig. 44.

Repeat the attack and when in position behind the opponent (Fig. 45) press your groins forcibly against his hips after having tightened your clasped hands as usual.

Figs. 47 and 48 show the succession of movements leading to the known finish shown in Fig. 42.

Repeat twenty times and then let your opponent do the same.

Now let yourself be attacked, the knife arriving at your throat and then at your abdomen, alternating the two until you are willing to let your opponent take your place.

You should be able by now to parry a straight right to your jaw. Examine Figs. 37, 38 and 39 and you will see that the only difference between a straight right punch to your jaw and the knife thrust is that the punch approaches you faster than the knife. But if you followed the instructions, your movements ought to be smooth and therefore swift enough to avoid the punch. Anyway, try it slowly at first, then gradually work up to normal speed.

It is more common to speak about a straight left to the jaw, and this reminds us that we must learn how to parry a knife thrust delivered with the left hand.

**This is very important for there are many more people left-handed when using a knife than when doing anything else, for handling knives is not taught by parents at home, nor by teachers at school, so that the number of people who are likely to hold the knife in their left hand is relatively important.**

Read pages 38 and 39 again (Fourth Lesson) and note carefully that the lock is to be performed as usual by throwing your right arm around the opponent's neck and not otherwise as you may be inclined to do.

Try to push the attacking left elbow over to your left, sliding forward with your right foot. Here it is even more important than before to break very readily the contact of your right hand with the opponent's elbow, as you need it for the lock as soon as possible.

After you and your opponent have repeated a sufficient number of times, try the knife thrust at the region of the abdomen, delivered equally with the left hand.

You will find no difficulty now in parrying a straight left. This being tried as many times as necessary until you feel conversant with the movement, give your opponent also the opportunity of learning it.

# SIXTH LESSON

*Defense Against Alternate Left & Right Attacks, Understand Timing*

**REHEARSE** rapidly the previous lesson.

You will find no difficulty now in parrying an uppercut delivered with the right or the left. To make sure, just try methodically, slowly to begin with, gradually speeding up to normal action. Twenty trials with the right hand and as many with left are enough.

Now alternate attacks. Let your opponent try to hit you first with his right then with his left, then again with his right. All the movements with the fist should now be rehearsed in this way.

This being judged adequately done and with satisfactory results, but on no account otherwise, let your opponent attack you regularly and rhythmically with either hand as he chooses, the movements being regular but the alternation at his choice.

**Exercise these and you will soon find out that you know, an instant before the blow is delivered, with which hand it will be done.**

There is, of course, no use in going through the knife attacks alternating right and left. You push over to the side the hand thrusting the knife and that is that. **You do not move while the assailant does the actual action of killing.**

It might be profitable to make clear a basic principle underlying Judo, the present lessons being on similar lines. A **Samourai fable** will serve this purpose without abstract speculations.

A famous expert in the art wished to find out who among his disciples had grasped his teaching most fully. He gathered them and asked the following question.

"Imagine your sleep disturbed by the noise of footsteps which you realise to be those of your declared enemy. You then hear him cautiously opening the door. He is armed; he glides stealthily into the room, shuts the door to prevent the half light of dawn from waking you up and then proceeds noiselessly towards you. Knowing what you do, what is the precise moment you would rise to attack and destroy your enemy? Can you explain your choice? "

Try to answer the old man before learning the reply of his favourite pupils, which made him so happy that he did not mind departing for a better world. Anyway, so runs the story.

The answer that made the master happy was, that the assailant should be attacked while he is shutting the door.

The justification of this is that before shutting the door the assailant is all attention and may take up a different line of action as circumstances change. He may even give up for the time being and look out for another opportunity.

**After shutting the door the odds are too much in his favour considering the recumbent position of the victim.**

But he will not shut the door until he is satisfied that everything is all right. Thus, while shutting the door, his mind moves from caution to the conviction that he has cornered his prey. He has trapped his victim and is so sure of it that he will probably not mind his victim now waking up, once the door is shut behind him. So before this is accomplished, and while he is engaged in this action, attack him. This is the moment! **Take him unaware at the very moment when he is about to relax, due to the feeling of safety creeping into his mind.** This is your chance, for now he is most vulnerable.

If you examine all the illustrations you will see that the **attack is made on the assailant at the moment his action is irrevocable; when he is most sure of his prey.** The reason for that is now clear. Before the act of killing is undertaken he can feint, or change his mind. You must attack while he plunges his knife with weight and determination, not before. Of course, afterwards is too late so that you must time your attack at the correct moment. If you have been following the instructions and practicing them, you will certainly feel which is the right

moment. You must attack when the assailant is engaged in an action which he believes to be final.

You will know what he is going to do the next instant and the exact position of his body as though he were motionless.

The previous exercises were intended to put the body in a state of readiness to strike out at the right moment and make use of the only chance available.

It is easy to understand now why it has never been insisted that you should be swift. **There is no need to be swift, so long as your timing is correct.** The important thing is to act at the proper moment as described. Smooth action, clear thinking and, above all, practice will achieve far more than haste. This is important because you are going to use naked knives for further training, so you must go slowly.

Let your opponent attack you in slow motion to begin with, in all the ways of attack we have seen. At least twenty exercises should be done at every stage before going on to the next.

These repeated warnings may induce the idea of great danger. The danger is slight, but, **if one in a thousand of the exercises leads to an injury there will be a fair number of victims. There is no need to be scared stiff; to be careful is enough.**

Carry yourself easily, breathe normally and don't stiffen your muscles. It is astonishing how much more simply and easily one does things breathing freely and with the face relaxed, especially the lower jaw.

The purpose of training with bare weapons is not to learn anything new, nor to improve your speed, but to accustom you to the sight of the weapon, so that you maintain this relaxed and easy attitude in real combat. Without that attitude of mind and body all the speed you possess is of little practical avail.

# SEVENTH LESSON

*Overcome Attack with Bayonet from the Rear*

Fig. 49      Fig. 50      Fig. 51      Fig. 52

**THE** content of this lesson and the illustrations may not convince the reader. This is understandable because the result promised is difficult to believe. The fact is that it works. Those who follow the instruction, practicing regularly as advised, will find no difficulty in obtaining the result shown in Fig. 55, and this is all we are concerned with.

Let your opponent fix his bayonet with its scabbard on his rifle. Lift your hands, turn your back to him and let him thrust the end of his scabbard at your back. Such a situation can occur only if the opponent wants you to go ahead to a destination he has chosen. He uses his bayonet to urge you forward. You do not obey very readily. He certainly does not kill you - he could have done so before. He certainly wants you alive, for some time at least.

There is no choice left and you must obey. You advance, step by step. Try to do so in action, then examine Figs. 49 and 50 and then try again walking in front of the bayonet.

You will feel that starting with your right foot from the position shown in Fig. 49, which is the normal, usual and natural one, every time your right foot is advancing the contact with the scabbard is broken (see Fig. 50).

Repeat the movement and observe now that every time your right foot is advanced your hips are turned and your back, especially the part at which the bayonet may be applied, is not perpendicular or normal to the bayonet, but inclined.

In fact the angle is quite grazing and the smooth end of the

Fig. 53

Fig. 54

Fig. 55

scabbard will slide forward when pushed, as if on an inclined plane. Start afresh and try to produce a sufficient tension of your hips to make the scabbard end slip forward. You will see that a conscious movement hardly noticeable from that of normal walking is ample.

Now try again and when you feel ready, advance your right foot, half completing the shifting of your balance on to the advanced foot; complete the normal twist of your hips, while your left arm is lowered in a backward short swing to take you out of the way of the point of the weapon, and step with the left foot towards your opponent. Examine Fig. 51 and try again. It is easier to perform the movement if the right foot steps somewhat on the ball of the foot and the twist to the left is done

without letting the heel down heavily on to the ground.

Fig. 52 is taken in full action. Observe how simply the swing with left arm is done, and the longer step with the left foot. The man behind you has now set his mind on pushing forward his weapon, and he cannot check this tendency, nor the inertia of his body moving forward. Fig. 52 shows how natural it is for him to complete the started pace even if only to bring his left foot nearer to the right. Do not act jerkily and he will do this and so come into the best position to enable you to throw your right arm round his neck in the usual way as shown in Fig. 53; finish as shown in Figs. 54 and 55. You should of course proceed so that the result is obtained independently of the opponent completing his pace or not.

Fig. 49

Fig. 50

Fig. 56

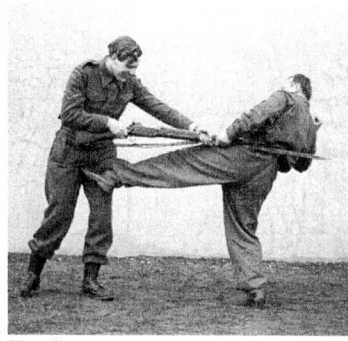

Fig. 57

Repeat a dozen times, then read the text again, and above all attentively scrutinise the illustrations, then proceed with another twenty repetitions.

Any movement of the body when described sounds complicated. That is where demonstration is a great help as it brings everything into a clear perspective. However, after a few trials you should succeed in fusing all the details into a simple purposeful action.

This movement helps you to turn the tables on your otherwise complete master in a situation from which you could hardly imagine escape to be possible. Moreover you, unarmed, can bring in a prisoner. So after your opponent has gone through the exercises repeat as many times as you can.

In action, some may argue, this is a very risky enterprise. No doubt it is, but after a hundred repetitions you will find yourself prone to argue to the contrary. The thing to remember is that in a position like that shown in Fig. 49 your life is not worth much unless you are prepared to talk and buy your own life at the cost of many of your comrades.

Let us now see the incidental difficulties that may arise in practice due to imperfect action or circumstances. The point of the bayonet is sharp and will not slip forward even when hardly in contact with your back. If you misjudged the distance or if for any other reason you turned to your left too soon, the bayonet tending forward will penetrate through the clothes, grazing your body. It may even wound you, though obviously this cannot be very serious as the weapon is skimming your body.

Should this happen or, as it did once in training in the conditions shown in Fig. 56, where the scabbard slid through the belt loop, you cannot apply the usual neck lock, as you are prevented from completing the turn of your body. Take hold of the rifle as shown in the Fig. 56, put your right foot short on the ground, lifting the left foot off the ground. To get the right idea of how the movement is done look back to Fig. 51 and imagine Fig. 56 being the continuation of it.

From standing on your left foot, Fig. 51, stamp your right forcibly down in place of the left foot lifted off the ground; it is somewhat of a hop from one foot to the other.

The body should be kept straight in the hips, the head and shoulders thrown back to the right corner so that your left thigh is horizontal (Fig. 67 shows this instant clearly) and shoot out your left foot from the knee as shown in Fig. 57.

It is obvious that you cannot try out the effect of the last act even if your movement is smooth and you must take great care that it does not happen by itself through slackened attention or excessive playfulness. Try a dozen times and change positions as customary.

# EIGHTH LESSON

*Alternative Movements Against Bayonet Attack from the Rear*

Fig. 49

Fig. 50

Fig. 51

Fig. 52

**REPEAT** the two movements of the last lesson.

The second movement was necessary because of a mechanical obstacle preventing you from turning sufficiently to your left. If for any reason your turning is delayed so that when it is completed you are in a position similar to that shown in Fig. 58, from which it is not handy to secure the usual lock on the neck, get hold of the rifle with your left hand (see illustration). Catch any part of his kit nearest to shoulder or as shown in Fig. 39. At the same time lift your right foot and stamp it down at the back of his left knee, pulling with your right hand in the direction of your right elbow.

Stamping your foot as shown in Fig. 60 will obviously dislocate the knee joint. In training press your foot progressively just behind the knee so as to bend it only, and force your opponent to kneel on it as in Fig. 61.

Great care must be taken not to be too efficient, especially if you are training in the village hall or similar place, where the wooden floor, intended to accommodate dancers, is slippery and likely to produce sprains. If in addition to the waxed floor you are wearing your iron clad boots, you have all that is necessary to get into trouble.

Having brought the opponent on to his knee, let go the hold with your right hand and throw it around his neck, securing the usual neck lock as in Fig. 61.

In training it is impossible to complete the movement, i.e., to bring the opponent on to his back so that his belt touches the

Fig. 58     Fig. 59     Fig. 60     Fig. 61

ground and then push his head forward as in Figs. 5, 14 or 16.

It is easy to realize that any further urge backwards applied to the kneeling man, in Fig. 61, unless purposely done so slowly as to enable him to disengage his left knee, will damage this beyond repair. In fact, even in action, there is no need to go further than securing the lock as in Fig. 61 if there is no other danger lurking near you.

Repeat slowly a dozen times.

On close examination of the figures you will notice that this last movement is possible only if the opponent pressed his bayonet forward, thus advancing his left foot as in Fig. 60.

If your movement is round, smooth and simple, as it should be if you have been practising properly all along, you may find yourself turning too rapidly, completing your rotation before the opponent has the leisure to realise what is happening. If this happens you will find yourself in the position shown in Fig. 62, where the opponent has hardly had time to move, let alone advance his left foot. Close your hand on the rifle as in the figure, bend your right elbow, bringing your right hand, held flat, towards your left shoulder and deal out a vigorous blow with the outer border of it against his throat at the Adam's Apple. (Fig. 63).

Pay attention to your left hand gripping the rifle. This act seems superfluous at first sight - it is on the contrary very important as it keeps your opponent away from you at a fixed distance. **Any attempt on his part to advance or to recede,**

Fig. 49     Fig. 50     Fig. 51     Fig. 52

**carries you with him, automatically keeping you at the best striking distance. It also makes the weapon as much yours as his.**

The blow must be a sharp and swift swing producing a cut as if with a sword. The soft padded edge of your hand between the small finger and wrist, is the part that comes in contact and produces the blow.

Needless to say, do not hit with any power unless your life is really at stake, for you may intend to deal just a little blow, but if your movements are anything like approaching natural speed of execution your opponent is tailing on to your hand with a certain velocity which you may not have taken into account.

Repeat a dozen times and change places with your opponent.

In the introduction it is pointed out that among the advantages of a unique movement are the restricted choice and the absence of having to make a decision before using it. On examining the four ways in which we have learned to attack an opponent forcing you forward at the point of his bayonet, namely, the normal neck lock, the kick, the knee crushing ending with a neck lock, and the last, the cut at the Adam's Apple, you may realise what was meant by difficulty of choice. **Which movement are you going to use? Will you make up your mind to use one of them before you start turning or will you turn and take a chance? These and other questions are probably creeping into your mind.**

There are two ways of settling them. **The first is training.**

Fig. 62          Fig. 63

But sufficient time must be allowed for that purpose, so that the movements become automatic. This solution will hardly satisfy you, neither does it go with the rapid "first-aid" course we set out to provide.

**The second is what I have adopted in practice.** Having tried the four different ways open to you after the twist of the body to the left, which puts you out of the way of the bayonet and closer to the opponent, so that another thrust is impossible, unless the opponent withdraws at least one pace, **make up your mind which of the four you prefer. Forget the others and practise only the one you prefer.**

My advice is to stick to the neck lock in the first place and learn the kick for a case of emergency only, as explained originally.

It should be borne in mind that if your opponent does not rely entirely on his weapon and tries to rid himself of it at the slightest pretext, he can take up a line of action similar to yours. That is why you should train, and the exercises were so devised that the shortest possible time elapses between your first move and the opponent's disablement. In practice a soldier parts with his weapon reluctantly, especially while making use of it, and unless he knows that it is a hindrance more than a weapon when attacking you, he will be loath to part with it. Moreover, if he does throw it away, equality of opportunity is achieved in an otherwise hopeless situation.

The value of what you have learned is thus standing out clearly: it is better than having a rifle and bayonet prodding at the back. You can hardly expect to achieve more than this.

# NINTH LESSON

*Defence Against Bayonet Attack from the Front*

Fig. 68    Fig. 64    Fig. 65    Fig. 66

**REPEAT** the movements of the previous lesson.

Stand facing your opponent, who tries to thrust his scabbard-covered bayonet into your stomach. Let him behave in a friendly mood while you are acquiring the rudiments of the movements. He can increase the weight of his attack when you have learned how to deal with it.

When the point of the bayonet is three or four inches from you, shift it over to your right as shown in Fig. 64, stepping forward somewhat to your left with your left foot.

Observe the figure and note the slight turn of the hips to your right. This again places your body in an inclined position relative to the weapon. It was perpendicular to your abdomen, when you faced your opponent; it is now almost parallel to the line of your shoulders in the Fig. 64.

Repeat this movement twenty times at least until you feel you can avoid the point of the scabbard even when your opponent tries hard to touch you.

Starting again from the facing position, hardly raise your heels from the ground in expectation of the thrust. Shift the weapon to your right as before with a short smooth swing of your arm, stepping forward with your right foot turned outwards as far as you can. Fig. 65 shows this position; note also that the contact with the weapon is made with the inside of the forearm, which is padded and can take quite a considerable shock without pain. If the opponent is small compared with yourself and you feel it more convenient for you, any part of the

Fig. 67           Fig. 67a

inside of the wrist, forearm or even the palm can be used. Note that the hand is held flat, the thumb along the other fingers. You must not, of course, try to take hold of the bayonet; all that is required is a mere push with a smooth swing of the left arm over to your right.

Bearing these remarks in mind, repeat the movement as shown in Fig. 65 several times and let your opponent take your place as usual.

Start again from the facing position, step forward with the right foot turned outwards, while shifting over the bayonet to the right (Fig. 65): bring your weight on to the right foot, and take hold of the rifle as shown in Fig. 66. Observe the position of the left arm after the bayonet has been deflected from its

course to your right. Note that the sooner you withdraw the left arm from following the rifle, once it is shifted, the easier it is to proceed.

Now try again, this time stamping down your right foot and raising your left leg as shown in Fig. 67. Observe the position of the body in the figure.

Try just to step into the position shown in Fig. 67 starting from normal standing position. Step forward with the right foot turned outwards (Fig. 65), stamping it forcibly on to the ground, lifting the left foot almost simultaneously to the position shown in Fig. 67. After a few trials you will find and appreciate the stability you gain through standing on one foot.

Having admitted the kick with the foot once in a previous lesson, there is no reason why we should not make the best of this movement. Little imagination is necessary to see that stretching the raised leg will bring the point of the foot against a very sensitive part of the opponent's body and will make him unfit for further combat (Fig. 67a).

It seems hardly necessary to warn you against trying to kick out and hit your opponent with the foot even if only gently.

Repeat from the start a dozen times and then do the attacking for your opponent's benefit.

If you have examined the figures closely you will have certainly noticed that in Fig. 67 the man thrusting the bayonet

Fig. 68    Fig. 69    Fig. 70

throws out his left foot forward, whereas in Fig. 65 it is his right foot that does it.

Both are possible, and in fact taught in bayonet training. You will find, however, that most people using the bayonet step with the left foot forward, which is the case shown in Figs. 64, 65, 66 and 67.

To meet the other case let your opponent thrust his weapon stepping forward with his right foot as in Fig. 68, from which you learn also that little is changed in your proceedings, that you still shift the weapon over to your right, stepping out with your left foot.

Fig. 69 shows the continuation of your movement, shifting your balance on to your left foot while the right hand takes

hold of the rifle; after that Fig. 70 is self-explanatory, showing again the well balanced position on one foot.

Repeat this last movement several times and let your opponent attack regularly, alternating the thrust, once with his left foot forward and next with his right foot forward. Then do the same for him.

The movements of this lesson are easy and effective, as you have satisfied yourself, even if the man with the bayonet attacks as swiftly as he can, but starts only a pace or two from you. Such a situation presents itself when being challenged by an opponent or otherwise being surprised by him.

If on the other hand the opponent dashes at you from a distance, gathering speed and momentum, the weight of his attack

Fig. d

Fig. e

makes it more and more difficult to maintain balance while kicking and frequent misses occur. If you happen to know other methods of parrying a bayonet thrust try them out in these extreme conditions of speed and dash. You will probably arrive at the same conclusion to which experience has led me, i.e., they become more or less ineffective.

It does not follow that an instructor or a well trained man is bound to fail, as body and the mind are influenced by long experience and he might succeed where you fail; so does the trapeze artist after long training. Even then most of them die sooner or later just because they missed their trick only once and just by a fraction of an inch.

Ordinary people are unable to persevere although they know they ought to and decide to. Tricks that need long and continuous training are in their case as useless as if they did not exist.

Now try this; let your opponent dash at you from four or five paces away. Be ready to move forward and to your left, while knocking the bayonet over to your right, as in Fig, 64, with open hand as customary, and secure our fundamental lock on his neck with your right forearm thrown around it as usual.

It may sound impracticable on first reading, yet it works with most people who have followed the instructions and practised all along as shown. The opponent when really dashing forward advances at least one pace while his bayonet is knocked out of your way, then stops, "waiting" for your lock on his undefended neck.

**Experience derived from actual training of units, shows that on the ninth lesson, after a few trials the number of successes rapidly approaches the number of attempts.**

Try then a dozen times and then let your opponent start dashing from farther away until he reaches a point where distance does not add anything to the weight of his attack. As usual give him a chance too. (See Fig. c and Fig. d)

# TENTH LESSON

*Defense Against Deviated Attack and Variations on Hadaka-Jime*

Fig. 68                    Fig. 64                    Fig. 65                    Fig. 66

**REPEAT** the last lesson a dozen times each movement.

Look back at Fig. 65. It is easy to infer that a well-trained man could, on finding the point of his bayonet deviated by your left arm, make use of the butt of his rifle and knock you on your head or face with it. During the exercises of the last lesson you may have found that you could do so.

Knowing what the unarmed victim is going to undertake, following up with a hard hit of the butt as attempted in Fig. 71 is almost spontaneous.

In practice such a possibility is almost excluded; at least it is highly improbable that a man thrusting his bayonet at an unarmed man is mentally prepared to fail and have to defend himself. Even if he succeeded in realising the danger, he has too short notice for action.

We have learned to stamp the right foot and kick with the left simultaneously or almost, so as to meet and forestall such action.

Nevertheless, in fighting, even the highly improbable may happen and we are going to act so that nothing is left to chance.

Observe Figs. 66 and 67 and note the position of the left arm of the defender. If for any reason the kick is late or misplaced and the butt is swung at you as in Fig. 71, turn the palm of your left hand towards the opponent and check its movement with the fleshy, padded part of the forearm.

We have already explained on a previous occasion that this part of the arm can withstand quite a hefty shock without damage or pain.

Fig. 71

Fig. 72

Fig. 73

To make sure of this, let your opponent try to hit you as shown in Fig. 71. Check his movement as described. Let him go easy while you get the knack of turning the palm and forearm towards the butt so that the inside of the forearm comes in contact with the weapon. Be careful in the first trials, for should the butt meet the ulna the weaker of the two will break. If you turned your forearm properly as shown in Fig. 71 and brought it against the butt so that the brunt of the impact is carried by the middle of the forearm as shown in Fig. 73 you will find after a few trials that you can check the full swing of any powerful knock without damage.

Try a dozen times until you know that you can do it; again, being careful to avoid the impact of the weapon at the bony parts of your forearm, i.e., wrist and elbow.

Now let the opponent thrust his bayonet forward and follow up with a blow of the butt to your head as in Fig. 71. Proceeding as usual, push the bayonet over to your right (Fig. 65), stepping forward with your right foot, the toes being turned outwards (see Fig. 66). It has been insisted, in the previous lesson, that you should push over the bayonet with a short sharp swing of the left forearm and immediately lift it to the position shown in Fig. 65, the right hand taking hold of the rifle. You are thus prepared automatically for the next move of your opponent, however unlikely it may be.

Check the falling blow as in Fig. 72 and finish as in Fig. 73. After a few trials you will find no difficulty in parrying the attack with the butt at your head even if your opponent only

Fig. 74

Fig. 75

Fig. 76

feints thrusting the bayonet and relies mainly on the blow of the butt to destroy you.

To complete the wide and various possibilities of the neck lock let your opponent go on all fours and approaching from behind, his right, or his left as in Fig. 74, throw your forearm round his neck as shown in Fig. 75, tighten your lock and roll over his right shoulder to find yourself in the familiar position shown in Fig. 76.

Be careful to tighten your arms before weighing over to the right so that you roll over and do not fall on your side without your opponent with you, for if this happens, not only will you be unable to carry out your intention but you will fall heavily on your right hip.

The application of the neck lock in such conditions may be useful in case your opponent falls from the sky near enough for you to close up before he disentangles himself from his parachute and fires at you.

If his head is nearest to you it would of course be a waste of precious time to turn round into the position of Fig. 74. Slide your right arm under his chin, bending your knees so as to make your abdomen press the top of his head as shown in Fig. 77.

Repeat this movement, pressing with your right wrist against his throat, while sliding it under his chin, so that when this is done his head is twisted as shown in the illustration. This result is achieved only if your abdomen exerts constant

Fig. 77          Fig. 78          Fig. 79

pressure on the top of his head, while sliding your right arm into position.

It is difficult to show the position of the wrist under his chin in the circumstances, but it is easy to understand that it is the hard, bony edge of the radius that bears against his throat.

Clasp your hands in the usual manner as shown in Fig. 78, tighten your arms and he is forced to lift his hands from the ground. If your abdomen presses on the top of his head as in the illustration the lock is already proving its effect.

Note the twisted position of his head, his eyes and face turned to your left. If you have not achieved this twist you had better start afresh until you have done so, then lift him from the ground by pushing your hips forward so as to increase the pres-

sure on his head, at the same time straightening your body to the vertical position, with your arms held tightly to your body.

Even if he caught hold of you as shown in Fig. 79, or in any other way, he cannot do very much to save his neck from being broken, if you find it necessary to do so. Should he try to pull at your ankles in order to make you fall, a sudden effort of your body backwards and of the abdomen downwards will make this his last deed.

You must be very careful not to obtain a similar result while training, therefore grip tightly, but don't stiffen your hold nor the body too suddenly. In short, exert the usual control over your movements.

Repeat the movement from the beginning a dozen times

73

and change places with your opponent.

Now, if for any unforeseen reason it happened that your opponent succeeded in getting you off your balance (which is difficult and therefore highly improbable as you had convinced yourself in your last exercises) just roll on to your back, wrap your legs around his waist, hook them and push your hips forward. The result is obvious from the first trial.

The roll on the back, the wrapping of the legs and the hooking are similar to those you have learned previously. Looking back at Figs. 6, 7 and 8 may prove to be useful.

This is the end of our introductory or, as we called it, "first-aid" course. **I hope I have convinced you of the importance of slow and thoughtful repetition.**

**So after some time has elapsed read the text once more; you will discover many important details that you have either discarded as non-essential, superfluous or pedantic, or simply overlooked;** then go through the whole course again, this time in full kit.

**An introductory course is obviously a limited one. Many questions that a little practice will answer or eliminate altogether were deliberately not touched.**

Others, more favourable to our method, were treated likewise. For instance, nothing was said about the effectiveness of the lock applied as shown in Figs 5, 14, 43, 55 and others, against opponents heavily clad in winter clothes, thick furs, several pairs of thick socks and felt or fur-padded jack-boots, as used on the Russian front in winter time. Punching, kicking or elaborate locks and twists are obviously not of any use here, while the neck lock is as effective as ever.

# AFTERWORD

**NOW**, after reading the book, and maybe trying some of the lessons, it is apparent that the theme of learning found in *Practical Unarmed Combat* is many repetitions of a movement. The practice of a movement, which becomes easier and more comfortable with each repetition, embeds the movement in the central nervous system. Once the movement is learned and accepted by the brain, the action is available without requiring a conscious effort to retrieve it.

It is obvious that he designed the course so that the trainees eventually repeated the core movement a thousand times, but much more was hidden in the process of learning. The designing of the training was tricky.

The process of learning the one effective core technique develops the ability to perform many techniques, to understand the principles of confronting an attacker with the correct state of mind, to gain the freedom to learn more.

Extreme knowledge and experience are needed to pull off this kind of trick; to see the whole picture and visualize all stages of learning – from the most basic to the culmination – choosing the technique and providing the ability to perform it in a crisis situation. Thus the trainees learned a whole system of self defense.

I would like to mention the parallels I found between this book and the martial arts classic literature. We can easily see that Moshe's instruction is consistent with the principles found in books such as *The Art of War*[26] and *The Book of Five Rings*.[27]

I believe that *Practical Unarmed Combat* by Moshe Feldenkrais is equal in stature and importance to works of this nature, which present the reader with immutable principles. In my opinion, *Practical Unarmed Combat* surpasses these classics because not only does it expound immutable principles, but it also offers practical techniques and a structured training process, which I have proven successful. Of course, it was necessary to make some minor changes to allow for modern weapons and today's environment.

The importance of principles/techniques learning is emphasized in another classic – *The Unfettered Mind* – stating that "Techniques and principles are just like two wheels of a cart."[28] Musashi also said: "The true Way of Martial Arts is in training in a way that it will be useful at any time and in teaching so it will be useful in all things". Moshe Feldenkrais' work transcends practical self defense, using unarmed combat as a vehicle to provide a method for learning and teaching.

## AFTERWORD

The heart of the *Feldenkrais Method* is the mind/body connection through action. Dr. Feldenkrais believed that, whereas the body and mind are an inseparable whole, the improvement of physical functioning through movement influences not only physical capabilities, but affects emotional and intellectual capabilities and the entire self.

# ABOUT
# MOTI (MORDEHAI) NATIV

Moti (Mordehai) Nativ, a retired colonel from the Israel Defense Forces, is a certified teacher of the Feldenkrais Method and Martial Arts.

Moti has graduated from the Jerusalem 1 Feldenkrais Professional Practitioner training in 1994 and served as the president of the Israeli Feldenkrais Guild.

Moti began studying Martial Arts in 1966, and his martial arts practice includes wrestling, Judo and Krav Maga. He holds a black belt in Judo, and he is a certified Krav Maga instructor.

Moti is Dai Shihan (master teacher) of Bujinkan school of Budo TaiJutsu. He is a member of this school since 1975, and since 1995 he has led the training of Bujinkan teachers in Israel. He founded the Bujinkan Shiki (Awareness) Dojo.

Moti has explored the peculiar way that brought Moshe Feldenkrais from the Land of Israel to become a Judo Master in France and England and the influence of the Martial Arts on the development of the Feldenkrais Method.

Moti teaches advanced workshops called, "The Synergy of Martial Arts and the Feldenkrais Method" worldwide.

Moti republished Moshe Feldenkrais's book Practical Unarmed Combat (originally published in 1942) and was involved in republishing Higher Judo (1948) and Autosuggestion (1929). Lately, he published an article about Moshe's unique work Better Judo (1948-1949).

# APPENDIX
## *Additional Photos*

Preparing the photo shoot.

# Defence Against Knife Attack

 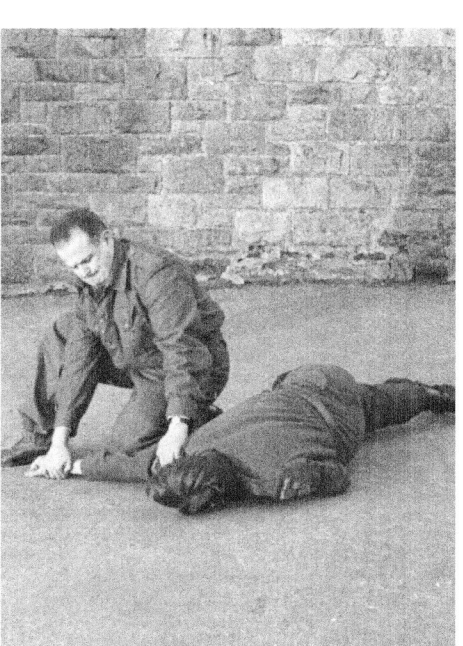 

*Moshe Feldenkrais training with Mr. Mikinosuke Kawaishi, his Judo Teacher and colleague at the Club Jiu-Jitsu de France*

# The Training Site

# NOTES

1. Amiel (Emil) Avineri was then the regional boxing champion, and was Moshe's training partner. Emil appears in many photos of the Jiu-Jitsu book.

2. **Haganah** - (Hebrew - pronounced "hah gah **nah**") Hebrew for "defense" was an underground organization first conceived in January 1920 and officially founded June 1920 during the British Mandate for Palestine, to protect the Jewish Yishuv (settlement) from Arab riots and violence. The official name was "Irgun Hahagannah Haivri" - The Jewish Defense Organization. The Haganah doctrine stressed loyalty, secrecy, and devotion to humanitarian and Jewish values including the sanctity of life. It became the unofficial army of the Jewish Agency. The nucleus of its leadership was taken from the Zionist socialist movements and the kibbutzim, and was a model of a citizens' army. The Haganah merged into the Israel Defense Forces (IDF) following the foundation of the state of Israel in May1948. Moshe Feldenkrais was a member of the Haganah during its pre-state period.

3. From *Moshe on Moshe on the Martial Arts,* The *Feldenkrais* Journal, 2:1, 1986, 14-19. "The British, if the book fell into their hands and they knew that I wrote it, they would probably arrest me and ask me who the leaders of the Haganah were and so on. So the day the book was published, I was in France."

4. Michel Brousse, *Les racines du judo français - Histoire d'une culture sportive,* Presses Universitaires de Bordeaux, pages 200-207.

5. Professor Kano described Judo as "...a mental and physical discipline whose lessons are readily applicable to the management of our daily affairs. The fundamental principle of Judo--one that governs all techniques of attack and defense--is that whatever the objective, it is best attained by the maximum-efficient use to mind and body for that purpose. The same principle applied to our everyday activities leads to the highest and most rational life."

6. From *The Principle of Judo is Like the Nature of Water* (Gunji Koizumi, 1885-1965): Dr. M. Feldenkrais has made a serious study of the subject, himself attaining Black Belt efficiency. He has studied and analyzed Judo as a scientist in the light of the laws of physics, physiology, and psychology, and he reports the results in this book which is enlightening and satisfying to the scientific mind of our age. Such a study has been long awaited and is a very valuable contribution to the fuller understanding and appreciation of the merits of Judo. Dr. Feldenkrais explains how Judo training educates one to be "independent of heritage." This phrase is the keynote and hallmark of the standard of his treatise. It is universally recognized that judo practice promotes the sense of balance and self-confidence, and cultivates the ability to overcome brute force and inherited weaknesses or shortcomings. But the logical and scientific reasons for these effects were left unexplored. Dr. Feldenkrais, with his learned mind, keen observation, and masterly command of words, clarifies the interrelation and the intermingled working of gravitation, body, bones, muscles, nerves, consciousness, subconscious and unconsciousness, and opens the way for better understanding.

7. The *Feldenkrais Method* aims to improve people's actions by increasing awareness of their movement through the use of verbal guidance or through gentle manipulation. The benefits are achieved by expanding their self-image so that they might include alternative options in their activities. It is particularly helpful to those suffering from limiting or adverse physical conditions.

8. *Hadaka-Jime: Practical Unarmed Combat,* page 11

9. From 1918-1950, before the declaration of the *Feldenkrais Method* and its two major techniques (*Functional Integration* and *Awareness Through Movement*), Moshe was active as a martial artist and was creative in that field. My claim is that while Moshe was devising his own self defense meth-

od, learning and teaching Judo, he used techniques, concepts and ideas that later became the ground for the *Feldenkrais Method*. Thus the *Feldenkrais Method* does have folded within it all of the principles of survival and self-defense. The "Synergy" research covers those early years in Moshe's life, focusing on his activities as a martial artist, analyzing his concepts and fighting techniques and their influence and appearance in the *Feldenkrais Method*.

The research covers Moshe's activities as a martial artist in Israel, France, England and Japan. Some findings of the "Synergy" research are already presented in this book, others will be presented in a new edition of the Jiu-Jitsu book (published in 1931), and finally I'll publish the complete work *Warrior's Awareness - The Synergy of Martial Arts and the Feldenkrais Method*.

10. "For physical education to be truly effective, it must be based on the principle of efficient use of mental and physical energy. I am convinced that future advances in physical education will be made in conformity with this principle" - Jigoro Kano

11. *Hadaka-Jime: Practical Unarmed Combat,* page 14

12. *Hadaka-Jime: Practical Unarmed Combat,* page 20

13. Dr. Hatsumi is the founder and the Soke (Grand Master) of Bujinkan School, that gathers the knowledge of nine ancient Japanese Martial Art systems.

14. You can read more about the Hadaka-Jime technique in the Kodokan formal Judo books: *Illustrated Kodokan Judo,* page 145 (by Dainippon Yubenkai Kodansha, Tokyo, 1955), *Kodokan Judo,* page 120 (edited by the Kodokan Editorial committee, 1986), and *Judo Formal Techniques* (*The Complete Guide to Kodokan Randori no Kata*), pages 330 -338 (published by Charles E. Tuttle Company, Inc, 1983)

15. *Hadaka-Jime: Practical Unarmed Combat,* page 39

16. *Hadaka-Jime: Practical Unarmed Combat,* page 20. In 1929 Moshe Feldenkrais translated the *The Practice of Autosuggestion* – the method of Emile Coué – to Hebrew. He added two chapters to the book to clarify his own understanding of the Autosuggestion. There he emphasized the importance of the unconsciousness for self-preservation. "With consciousness surely that not all would move in the same manner and not all are capable and skilled to come to the same decision. But the Unconsciousness is the Treasure of Memories and Experience, not only ours, also of our parents and the parents' parents, so through many generations of trial and error, this defense movement, was fixed this way, that will do it in spite of our conscious will."

17. Miyamoto, "A skillful person may appear slow, but he is never off the beat. No matter what a well-trained person does, he will never appear hurried."

18. From the article "The Walking Stick in Mandatory Palestine and Israel" (by my friend, the martial arts researcher Noah Gross). "KAPAP stands for Krav panim-el-panim, literally translates into face-to-face combat. A variety of disciplines were taught under this heading, among them: Judo, Jujitsu, Boxing, Knife, stone throwing and the Walking stick and short stick methods. With time the name came to be associated primarily with the stick fighting methods". (The full article can be viewed at http://lacannevigny.wordpress.com/israel-connection/)

19. These lectures led to the publication of *Body & Mature Behavior* in 1949.

20. *Hadaka-Jime: Practical Unarmed Combat,* page 41

21. *Hadaka-Jime: Practical Unarmed Combat,* page 60

22. *Hadaka-Jime: Practical Unarmed Combat,* page 42

23. *Hadaka-Jime: Practical Unarmed Combat,* page 47

24. *Hadaka-Jime: Practical Unarmed Combat,* page 21

25. See *Judo*, pages 141-143. Frederick Warne & Co., Ltd.

26. Sun Tzu (6th century BCE)

27. Miyamoto Musashi, (1584- 1645) founder of Niten Ryu

28. *The Unfettered Mind* - Writings from the Zen Master Takuan Soho (1573-1645) to Yagyu Munenori a Master Swordsman. "There is such thing as training in Principle, and such a thing as training in Technique. If you do not train in Technique but only fill your breast with Principle, your body and hands will not function. Training in Technique, if put into terms of your own Martial Art, is in the training that if practiced over and over again makes the five body postures one. Even though you know principle, you must make yourself perfectly free in the use of technique. And even though you may wield the sword that you carry with you well, if you are unclear on the deepest aspects of principle, you will likely fall short of proficiency. Techniques and Principles are just like two wheels of a cart."

# ACKNOWLEDGEMENTS

Thanks to Mrs. Leah Smaller for translation, editing, and her important advice along the way. My thanks to Lori Mitchell for fine tuning and to my dear teachers and friends for taking the time to comment and assist with clever inputs: Yochanan Rewerant, Dr. Smadar Peleg, Shihan Roy Wilkinson, Shidoshi Roger Chaot, Ashley Bronzan, Lynnet Bannion, and Dr. Ronit Zilberman. Finally, thanks to Al Wadleigh for his professional work and for taking the risk of publishing this book.

# RESOURCES

For information about *Feldenkrais* products, classes, courses,
articles and other resources:
The *Feldenkrais* Store
AchievingExcellence.com

For information about *Feldenkrais* in Practice, Moti Nativ's
Method visit: Feldenkrais-IP.org

For information about *Feldenkrais Method, Feldenkrais*
practitioners and professional trainings, contact the *Feldenkrais*
*Guild* of North America:
FeldenkraisGuild.com

To find *Feldenkrais* practitioners and classes in your area visit:
Feldenkrais.com

The Israeli *Feldenkrais* Guild: Feldenkrais-Israel.org

International *Feldenkrais* Federation:
Feldenkrais-Method.org

Printed in Great Britain
by Amazon